Everyday American Idioms for ESL Learners

STEPHEN LAU

DEDICATION

This book is dedicated to those who wish to learn and know more about American English, especially to those whose English is not their first language.

INTRODUCTION

Idioms are words and phrases in a language that have come into existence for a variety of reasons, some obvious enough, some inexplicable, but most of them appropriately and delightfully characteristic of the race that created them. American idioms are no exception; they reflect American culture at every social level. They are used in everyday life, in speaking and in writing, in movies and on television, and by people from all walks of life. Some of the American idioms may be unfamiliar even to some Americans, especially ESL (English as a Second Language) learners.

There are approximately nine-hundred American idioms selected in this book for ESL learners to provide them with a better understanding of American English. Learn them so that you may know what they mean when they are used by Americans, and use them in their right context in your speaking and writing in your daily contacts with Americans.

Each American idiom comes with a simple explanation followed by one or more examples, showing you how to use it. Make an effort to learn ten American idioms a day, and then review what you have learned over the weekend. Then proceed to learning another ten, and so on and so forth. You may not remember all the American idioms that you have learned, but, rest assured, they will come back to you when you hear them in your social contacts with Americans.

Learning American idioms is as important as learning the vocabulary, the sentence structure, and the grammar usage of American English. If you plan to stay in the United States, learning American idioms is a must.

Stephen Lau

"A"

Abide by: accept and follow rules and regulations

e.g. If you wish to become a citizen of the United States, you must **abide by** U.S. immigration laws.

Above all: most importantly

e.g. **Above all**, you must have a valid visa if you wish to continue to stay in the United States.

Above and beyond: more than what is required or expected

e.g. Asking the employees to work extra hours but without paying them is **above and beyond** their loyalty.

Accountable for: responsible for; able to explain why

e.g. As an adult, you are **accountable for** your behavior.

e.g. You have to be **accountable for** every decision you are going to make.

Ace it: pass a test with an A grade; surpass someone in a competition e.g. I knew I would **ace** my test, and I did!

e.g. Peter **aced** Paul in the spelling contest.

Act one's age: behave maturely

e.g. Stop behaving like a teenager! You are an adult now; **act your age**!

Actions speak louder than words: do something about it, not just talking about it

e.g. Show me what you have done! **Actions speak louder than words**.

Add insult to injury: make things worse, not better

e.g. Enough is enough! Don't **add insult to injury**!

After a fashion: somehow or somewhat

e.g. I play the piano **after a fashion**—well, not like a concert pianist.

After all: in spite of everything

e.g. She didn't get a good score; **after all**, it was her first attempt.

After hours: after normal working hours

e.g. We were so busy that many of us had to stay **after hours to** finish the work.

Afraid of one's own shadow: easily frightened

e.g. Don't tell her that this is an unsafe neighborhood; she is already **afraid of her own shadow**.

Against all odds: In spite of all the problems and difficulties

e.g. **Against all odds**, the scientist completed his research successfully.

A little bird told me: somehow I knew

e.g. "How did you know what I did?" "Well, **a little bird told me**."

Alive and kicking: living and healthy; okay

e.g. I had been sick for some time, but now I am **alive and kicking**."

e.g. "How are you?" "Well, **alive and kicking**."

All at sea: confused

e.g. The lawyer was **all at sea** when he read the two conflicting reports of the incident.

All in a day's work: part of daily work

e.g. I don't like to cook, but cooking is **all in a day's work**.

All of it: the best

e.g. From the way he presented himself at the debate, he was **all of it**.

All systems are go: everything is good and ready as planned

e.g. Everything is in order, and **all systems are go**. We can now launch the project.

All thumbs: awkward and clumsy with one's fingers; not a handy person e.g. She will not learn to play the piano because she knows her fingers are **all thumbs**.

All wet: completely wrong

e.g. If you think I'm going to marry her, you're **all wet**!

Ankle: leave or quit work permanently

e.g. I told him he could **ankle** if he didn't like his job.

Anything but: not at all, not the least

e.g. I am **anything but** nervous about the driving test tomorrow.

e.g. You're telling me **anything but** the truth.

Armed to the teeth: heavily armed

e.g. The police were **armed to the teeth** to confront the rioters.

As blind as a bat: blind not seeing the truth

e.g. Everybody, except you, can see that he was the one who took the money. Are you **as blind as a bat**?

As clear as mud: not understandable; totally unclear; unintelligible

e.g. I had no idea what he was saying; his explanation was **as clear as mud**.

As comfortable as an old shoe: very comfortable

e.g. I like my old house; it was **as comfortable as an old shoe**.

As cool as a cucumber: calm and not easily agitated

e.g. You are always **as cool as a cucumber**; I like your temperament.

As different as day and night: very different

e.g. My brother and I are twins, but we are **as different as day and night**.

As easy as pie: very easy to do

e.g. Cooking a turkey is **as easy as pie**.

As far as it goes: as much as something does (usually negative in meaning)

e.g. **As far as it goes**, the project has not solved any of our problems.

As flat as a pancake: very flat

e.g. You left front wheel tire is **as flat as a pancake**.

As funny as a crutch: not funny at all

e.g. Your joke was **as funny as a crutch**; it fell flat, and nobody laughed.

As good as done: done, finished

e.g. As far as I am concerned, the mission is **as good as done**.

As good as gold: genuine, sincere

e.g. My words are **as good as gold**; just trust me!

As it were: as one might say

e.g. I was feeling, **as it were**, the winter blues, sad and depressed.

As I live and breathe: what a surprise; for sure, truly

e.g. **As I live and breathe**, I didn't expect to see you here, of all people!

e.g. **As I live and breathe**, you will be my wife and partner for the rest of my life.

As likely as not: probably

e.g. **As likely as not**, he will not come to the wedding.

As luck would have it: as it turned out; by chance

e.g. **As luck would have it**, we had a flat tire on our way to the wedding.

As plain as day: plain and simple

e.g. The briefing was as **plain as day**; nobody had to ask any question.

As sick as a dog: very sick

e.g. With the flu, I was **as sick as a dog** for days.

As the crow flies: straight across the land

e.g. Her house is just a few miles from downtown **as the crow flies**.

At a sitting: at one time; during one period

e.g. This restaurant can serve only 30 customers **at a sitting**.

At best: under the most favorable conditions

e.g. **At best**, we can finish only the minimum; at worst, we have to give up the whole project.

At loggerheads: in total disagreement

e.g. The two political parties have been **at loggerheads** since the election.

At loose ends: restless and unsettled; unemployed

e.g. Since he was diagnosed with depression, he has been **at loose ends**.

e.g. I have been **at loose ends** for more than a year since I lost my job at the restaurant.

At the drop of a hat: very ready; at any time

e.g. I am good and ready to go. I can leave **at the drop of a hat**.

At the eleventh hour: at the last possible moment

e.g. We nearly missed our flight when we got to the airport **at the eleventh hour**.

At the outside: at the most

e.g. To fix this computer, it should cost $40 **at the outside**; I won't pay anything more than that, if I were you..

At the ready: available for use

e.g. All the knives and forks are **at the ready** for the barbeque.

Attic: the head

e.g. You've got nothing in the **attic**!

e.g. He has an **attic** full of knowledge and wisdom.

Away from one's desk: not available

e.g. I'll be **away from my desk** the whole afternoon. Tell them to call back tomorrow.

"B"

Back to the drawing board: start planning all over again

e.g. Your plan didn't work. **Back to the drawing board** and start from scratch!

Bad rap: a bad reputation

e.g. This software has gotten a **bad rap**, and now nobody wants to use it.

Bad sort: an unpleasant person

e.g. He is a **bad sort**; nobody likes his company.

Bag your face: shut up!

e.g. You and your loud mouth! Go and **bag your face**!

Ball of fire: an energetic and enthusiastic person

e.g. We all want his presence at the party; he is a **ball of fire**.

Bang for the buck: value for the money spent

e.g. I didn't get anywhere near the **bang for the buck** for my secondhand car I purchased recently. It's a lemon!

Bank on: depend or rely on

e.g. My word is as good as gold; you can **bank on it**.

Bark up the wrong tree: make the wrong choice; accuse the wrong person

e.g. If you think I took your money, you're **barking up the wrong tree**.

Bashed: drunk

e.g. You were all **bashed** when you came home last night!

Beans: nonsense

e.g. Tell me the truth! No more **beans** from you!

Beat around the bush: do or say something indirectly

e.g. Don't **beat around the bush**! Tell me what's on your mind.

Beat a dead horse: continue a fruitless argument

e.g. The matter has now been settled. Why are you still **beating the dead horse**?

Be a breeze: very easy to do

e.g. All of you will pass the test; it will **be a breeze**.

Be caught flat-footed: be totally unprepared

e.g. Some public speakers are **caught flat-footed** when they cannot respond well to questions from the audience.

Be caught red-handed: be caught in the act of a crime

e.g. The thief with the stolen goods was **caught red-handed** when the police turned up.

Be down on one's luck: be out of luck; have no money

e.g. Please help me! I've been **down on my luck** for some time.

Be that as it may: although that may be true

e.g. He might be telling the truth. **Be that as it may**, nobody believed him!

Be the end of: be the cause of one's downfall

e.g. His gambling and drug addiction may well **be the end of** him.

Beat the clock: finish something before time is up

e.g. Time is running out. You have to work harder to **beat the clock**.

Become of: happen to

e.g. We haven't seen him for a while; what has **become of** his business?

Begin to see daylight: begin to see the end of a long task

e.g. Well, finally, we may **begin to see daylight**; the project is winding down.

Begin to see the light: begin to understand

e.g. After my briefing, he **began to see the light**; the project was not as simple as he had thought.

Believe it or not: it is true, whether you agree or disagree e.g. **Believe it or not**, she won the gold medal in the piano competition.

Beyond one's depth: too difficult for; not easy to understand

e.g. Algebra is **beyond my depth**; I'm thinking of dropping this subject.

Bet your bottom dollar: be confident of some fact

e.g. You can **bet your bottom dollar** that this is the truth, and nothing but the truth!

Between a rock and a hard place: between two equally difficult choices

e.g. Taking those medications with harmful long-term side effects or suffering those unbearable symptoms puts me **between a rock and a hard place**.

Beyond one's means: more than one can afford

e.g. Going on a cruise is **beyond my means**.

Beyond the pale: unacceptable; outlawed

e.g. Your behavior at the bar this evening was **beyond the pale**; it might have ended in your arrest by the authority.

Big gun: a powerful and influential person

e.g. He is a **big gun** in the committee.

Big noise: an important person

e.g. He is the **big noise** in Washington.

Bite one's nails: be anxious and nervous

e.g. We were **biting our nails** while you were in the surgery room.

Bite one's tongue: refrain from saying what one wants to say

e.g. He found it hard to **bite his tongue** when she was lying in her teeth.

Bite the dust: fall and die

e.g. The policeman fired the gun, and the young man **bit the dust**.

Blimp out: overeat

e.g. If you wish to manage your weight, don't **blimp out** on weekends.

Blow it: lose the opportunity

e.g. That was the opportunity of his life, but he **blew it** by not working hard enough.

Blow off: waste time

e.g. This work needs to be done; don't **blow off** too much!

Blow one's cool: become angry

e.g. I almost **blew my cool** when she insulted me with her remark.

Blow the whistle: reveal the secret

e.g. This will be a big scandal if somebody **blows the whistle** to the press.

Bone of contention: cause or source of disagreement

e.g. Racial discrimination is the **bone of contention** in this country.

Bone up on: study hard

e.g. If you want to pass your exam, you have to **bone up on** it.

Bread and butter: a person's income or livelihood

e.g. Mowing people's lawns is his **bread and butter**.

Break the bank: cost a fortune; ruin finance

e.g. Dining in that expensive restaurant won't **break the bank**.

Break the ice: start a social conversation

e.g. It's not easy to **break the ice** among all these strangers.

Bring something to light: make something known

e.g. We have to **bring the new evidence** to light so that the investigator may make a decision.

Buckle down: work hard and seriously

e.g. To get good grades, you have to **buckle down**.

Bum something: beg or borrow something from someone

e.g. Can I **bum** a dollar off you for my bus fare?

Bump up: promote

e.g. We expect the manager will **bump him up** because he is hard working.

Bury the hatchet: make peace; stop the conflict

e.g. The two political parties **should bury the hatch** and come to some compromise.

Busman's holiday: a holiday in which one has to work

e.g. It was only a **busman's holiday** for me; I still had many files that I had to go through while on vacation.

Butter up: excessively and insincerely praise someone

e.g. Don't try to **butter up** your parents; they won't let you have what you want.

Button one's lips: keep quiet and stay quiet

e.g. I am in the middle of something; can you **button your lips** and give me a break?

Buy a pig in a poke (a bag): buy something without seeing it

e.g. Making a purchase on the Internet is sometimes like **buying a pig in a poke**.

Buy it: die

e.g. When my car crashed, I thought I was going to **buy it**.

Buy something: believe

e.g. Nobody would **buy your story**, incredible as it is!

By leaps and bounds: increase rapidly

e.g. Ever since the company's makeover, its profits have increased by **leaps and bounds**.

By the same token: in the same way

e.g. I am nice to you; **by the same token**, I expect you to be nice to me.

By the skin of one's teeth: just barely

e.g. I did not miss my plane; I made to the airport **by the skin of my teeth**.

"C"

Cakewalk: something easy to do

e.g. There was nothing to it; it was just a **cakewalk**!

Call: a decision; a prediction

e.g. That was a good **call**; you did it right.

Call it a day: quit work and go home

e.g. I'm tired; let's **call it a day**.

Call it quits: quit for good

e.g. I've had enough; I'm **calling it quits**.

Call someone on the carpet: scold or reprimand

e.g. If you are late for work one more time, the manager will **call you on the carpet**.

Call the shots: make all the important decisions

e.g. In our company, it is the assistant manager who is **calling the shots**.

Can't argue with that: agree totally

e.g. You said the accident was intentional. I **can't argue with that**.

Can't complain: fairly good

e.g. Well, the result is as good as can be; just **can't complain**!

Can't do anything with: unable to manage

e.g. He just **can't do anything with** his daughter's eccentric behavior.

Can't make heads or tails of something: can't understand; have no clue

e.g. He is behaving so strangely lately. I just **can't make heads of tails** of him.

Can't say I do: no, I don't

e.g. "You don't like it?" "**Can't say I do**."

Carry the day: succeed, win

e.g. In a debate, the eloquent usually **carries the day**.

Case in point: an example; an illustration

e.g. Talking on the cell phone while driving is dangerous. A **case in point**, my neighbor had a car accident last week while talking on his cell phone.

Cast pearls before swine: give something of value to someone undeserving and unappreciative

e.g. If I were you, I wouldn't give it to him; he never

appreciates anything you give to him. Don't **cast pearls before swine**!

Catch one's death: catch a cold

e.g. Do come in, or you'll **catch your death**.

Caught short: be without something, such as money

e.g. My wife needed some eggs for her dessert, but she was **caught short**.

Change horses in midstream: change leaders or plans in the middle of a crisis

e.g. To replace the current CEO in this financial crisis is to **change horses in midstream**.

Chop: a rude remark

e.g. He made a **chop** about my makeup, and he didn't even apologize.

Chow down: eat

e.g. The puppy is always ready to **chow down** anything you give her.

Cock-and-bull story: something totally untrue; a lie

e.g. Don't give me this **cock-and-bull story**! You take me for a fool!

Cold cash: money not credit

e.g. Will you give me a better price if I give you **cold cash**?

Come again: please repeat

e.g. "I'm not going to help you." "**Come again**."

Come a cropper: fail, meet a misfortune

e.g. He invested all his money in the stock market. **He came a cropper** when the market crashed.

Come by: obtain

e.g. How did you **come by** this antique watch?

Come out of the closet: reveal one's deepest secret

e.g. The actor **came out of the closet**, and said he was gay.

Come to a head: come to a crucial point

e.g. The violence between the Israelites and the Palestinians are **coming to a head**.

Come to an untimely end: come to an early death

e.g. Due to cancer, the politician **came to an untimely end**.

Come to grips with: face something

e.g. It was a wakeup call for him; he began to **come to grips with** the reality of his future.

Come what may: no matter what

e.g. Don't worry! **Come what may**, I'll always be on your side.

Comer: a person with a bright future

e.g. He is a late **comer** in politics.

Cool one's heels: wait patiently

e.g. I told him to **cool his heels** until his name was called.

Cop out: back out of a duty or responsibility

e.g. He is most unreliable; he may **cop out**, leaving us to finish his work.

Cut and dried: already decided

e.g. The proposal is **cut and dried**; there is little we can do about it.

Cut something to the bone: cut severely

e.g. We have to **cut the budget to the bone** in order to save the company from bankruptcy.

Cut to the chase: get to the point; be concise and precise

e.g. I am the kind of person who will call a spade a spade: I like to **cut to the chase**.

"D"

Damage: cost

e.g. "What's the **damage** for this hat?" "Twenty dollars."

Dance to another tune: change to a different attitude or behavior

e.g. If your parents were here, you would **dance to another tune**.

Dawn on: become clear

e.g. It suddenly **dawned on** me that he was the one who secretly gave us the help we needed.

Dead and buried: gone forever

e.g. That was an ancient custom, **dead and buried** long time ago; nobody practices it any more.

Dead beat: a lazy person; a person who doesn't pay back debt

e.g. She is a **dead beat**; don't expect she'll ever pay you back the money.

Dead to the world: very tired

e.g. After working on the garden for hours, I am **dead to the world**.

Death on someone or something: harmful to

e.g. This road is so rough that it's **death on** car tires.

Deck out: dress up

e.g. They were all **decked out** for the July 4th party.

Deep pockets: very rich

e.g. He has **deep pockets**; maybe he can finance your education.

Dicey: uncertain of the outcome

e.g. The deal is a bit **dicey**—you know, touch and go.

Dig up: listen carefully

e.g. **Dig up**! He's going to give us all the details of the program.

Dish the dirt: gossip

e.g. Let's go and **dish the dirt** at the party.

Do a snow job on someone: deceive or confuse someone

e.g. Don't **do a snow job on** me! I know what you're up to.

Do someone in: kill someone

e.g. She always threatens to **do herself in** if I don't do what she asks.

Do something hands down: do something easily without much opposition

e.g. The Governor won his election **hands down**.

Do the dishes: wash the dishes

e.g. Who is going to **do the dishes** tonight? Not me!

Dog in the manger: a very selfish person

e.g. Don't be a **dog in the manger**! You no longer need this; why don't you give it to us?

Dollar for dollar: considering the amount of money spent

e.g. **Dollar for dollar**, I think that was a good deal.

Don't hold your breath: it might take longer than you think

e.g. At last the law might be passed by the Congress, but **don't hold your breath**.

e.g. I think she'll find a job soon, but **don't hold your breath**!

Don't I know it: I know it very well

e.g. "You have to get all the details before taking any action." "**Don't I know it**."

Don't look a gift horse in the mouth: be appreciative of any gift

e.g. You should be more thankful and less critical of the gifts from your friends; **don't look a gift horse in the mouth**.

Dose of one's own medicine: being treated the way one treats others

e.g. Now you're getting a **dose of your own medicine**—see how you like it!

Down and out: very poor

e.g. He is **down and out** without a job and a roof over his head.

Downbeat: cool, easygoing

e.g. He is such a cool guy—with a **downbeat** personality. I'm sure you'll like him.

Down in the dumps: sad and depressed

e.g. For months, she has been **down in the dumps**; she needs to see a doctor.

Down to the wire: to the last minute, to the very end

e.g. We are now **down to the wire** in this election. In the next hour or so, we will have a new President.

Draw a blank: find nothing; get no response

e.g. I tried to recall his name, but my mind **drew a blank**.

Drop the ball: make a mistake; fail in some way

e.g. I just can't rely on you to do anything. You always **drop the ball**.

Drop the other shoe: do the expected

e.g. They are now separated. Soon they will **drop the other shoe**, and file for a divorce.

"E"

Ear-duster: a person who likes to gossip

e.g. My neighbor is sort of an **ear-duster**, but she's all heart.

Early on: at any early stage

e.g. I started learning my piano **early on**.

Earn one's keep: help out with daily chores

e.g. You can stay with us, but you must **earn your keep** by doing the dishes.

Easier said than done: easy to say but difficult to do

e.g. Dog training is **easier said than done**.

Easy does it: go carefully and slowly

e.g. This TV set is very heavy, so **easy does it**.

Easy mark: a likely victim

e.g. There're many swindlers here. She's an **easy mark**, but I've warned her to be careful with her money.

Easy money: money easily earned

e.g. Well, that was **easy money**; I'm not sure if it's illegal.

Easy street: financial security

e.g. If you get that job, you will be on **easy street** for the rest of your life.

Eat like a bird: eat very little

e.g. My grandma, who is ninety years old. **eats like a bird**.

Eat like a horse: eat a lot

e.g. They won't invite you to dinner next time; just now you **ate like a horse**.

Eat one's hat: indicate something is most unlikely to happen

e.g. I'll **eat my hat** if he is elected Major!

Eat one's cake and have it: have everything one wants

e.g. You have to choose between this and that; you just **can't eat your cake and have it**.

Eat one's heart out: feel bitter

e.g. She still **eats her heart out** over what you said to her last night.

Eat out of someone's hand: be controlled by someone

e.g. Now that you are an adult, you still **eat out of your mother's hand**.

Eleventh hour: the latest possible time

e.g. We got to the airport at **the eleventh hour**, and didn't miss our plane.

End of one's rope: at the limit of one's patience

e.g. You're driving me crazy; I'm at the **end of my rope**.

Ends: money

e.g. Do we have enough **ends** to last through the trip?

Enough said: say no more

e.g. I don't want to hear anything from you. **Enough said**!

Every dog has his day: everyone will get a chance

e.g. Be patient! You'll be chosen for the team one day. **Every dog has his day**.

Every living soul: every person

e.g. **Every living soul** will have to be here on time because we are leaving at 8 a.m. sharp!.

Everything but the kitchen sink: almost everything one can think of

e.g. The burglar broke into the house and took **everything but the kitchen sink**.

Everything from soup to nuts: everything one can think of

e.g. At dinner, we were served **everything from soup to nuts**.

:

"F"

Face man: a good-looking guy with no personality or talent

e.g. He's just a **face man**, and no more. You want a man to have a brain, don't you?

Face-off: a confrontation

e.g. The demonstrators were heading towards a **face-off** with the police.

Face the music: confront danger; accept a bad situation

e.g. There are many circumstances in life in which one has to **face the music**.

Face up to: confront, deal with

e.g. You have to **face up to** your problems; you just can't run away from them.

Fade: leave

e.g. It's time to **fade**. See you tomorrow!

Fair and square: honestly and deservingly

e.g. I won the **competition fair and square**.

e.g. He earned his promotion **fair and square** with his excellent performance.

Fair to middling: so-so; okay, mediocre

e.g. "How is your health? "Well, **fair to middling**, I guess."

Fair shake: a fair bargain or opportunity

e.g. The boss always gives his employees a **fair shake** as far as promotion is concerned.

Fair-weather friend: dependable only in good times

e.g. Don't count on him; he is only a **fair-weather friend**.

Fall in place: fit together; provide a clear picture

e.g. With all the information in front of us, things now begin to **fall in place**.

Fall in with: agree with

e.g. They all **fell in with** our plans, and cooperated with us in the project.

Fall on one's face: make wrong judgment

e.g. Again, he **fell on his face** in predicting the winner in the competition.

Fall through: fail to complete

e.g. The proposal **fell through** due to insufficient facts and information.

Far cry from: very different from

e.g. Your achievement this time is a **far cry from** your previous one.

Fat chance: little chance, most unlikely

e.g. "You think he's going to win in the race?" "**A fat chance**!"

e.g. "Does he have a chance in this coming election?" "Yes, a **fat chance**!"

Feed the kitty: make a contribution

e.g. Please **feed the kitty** and help the homeless.

Feel like: have a desire for something

e.g. I **feel like** eating a hamburger.

Fight tooth and nail: fight hard

e.g. In the coming election, he is going to **fight tooth and nail** to get re-elected.

Fill someone's shoes: do someone's work

e.g. It's not easy to **fill your shoes** because you are so conscientious and efficient.

Find fault with: criticize

e.g. You always **find fault with** everything I do.

First and foremost: first of all

e.g. To lose weight, you must, **first and foremost**, stop eating junk food.

First and last: above all; under all circumstances

e.g. She was an accomplished pianist **first and last**.

Fish out of water: a person away from his or her comfort zone

e.g. In the company of politicians, I feel like a **fish out of water**.

Flag: fail a course subject

e.g. I **flagged** my algebra again.

Flash in the pan: only temporary success or accomplishment

e.g. His initial success was only a **flash in the pan**.

Flick: a movie

e.g. That was a pretty good **flick**; I enjoyed it very much.

Flip-flop: change sides in an issue

e.g. Politicians who **flip-flop** too much are unpopular with voters.

Flip side: the "other" side of something

e.g. The prosecutor would like to hear the **flip side** of the story before making a decision.

Float a loan: get a loan

e.g. I need money right now; I hope I can **float a loan** from you.

Fly in the ointment: something that spoils or prevents success e.g. Their new house is beautiful. The only **fly in the ointment** is their small kitchen.

Fly off the handle: lose self-control or temper

e.g. As soon as he heard the bad news, he **flew off the handle** and started screaming at everyone.

For a song: inexpensive

e.g. You can get this on the Internet **for a song**.

For that matter: as for that; as far as that is concerned

e.g. I was displeased by what he said. **For that matter**, I was angry.

Fork out: pay

e.g. I like this computer, but I don't want to **fork out** a lot of money for it.

Foul play: illegal activity

e.g. The police are investigating into the tragedy and suspected there was some **foul play**.

e.g. The whole incident looks too fishy to me, and I'm sure there must be some **foul play** involved.

From rags to riches: from poverty to wealth

e.g. His good fortune turned him **from rags to riches**.

From the bottom of one's heart: sincerely

e.g. **From the bottom of my heart**, I wish you all the best.

From the word go: from the start

e.g. I've had problems with my car **from the word go**.

Full of crap: talking nonsense all the time

e.g. I don't like your friend; he's **full of crap**.

"G"

Gang up on: join to attack; bully

e.g. They all **gang up on** the new student with verbal attacks.

Get a grip on: have control over one's behavior

e.g. **Get a grip on** yourself; everybody is staring at you.

Get a handle on something: get control or understanding of a situation

e.g. As soon as he heard the crisis, the President tried to put all the facts together to **get a handle on** the underlying cause of the crisis.

Get an in with: have influence with someone in authority

e.g. If you can **get an in with** the officials, you can park your car here.

Get down to brass tacks: get down to business or the basics e.g. There were far too many rumors. We had to **get down to brass tacks** in order to get to the bottom of the truth.

Get it: understand a joke or a point of information

e.g. Sorry, I didn't **get it**. Say that again.

Get nowhere: make no progress

e.g. Without your help, I am **getting nowhere** in this project.

Get one's feet wet: start a new venture

e.g. We're trying to **get our feet wet** in the retail business.

Get out of my face: go away and stop bothering me

e.g. Stop bothering me! **Get out of my face**!

Get real: be realistic and practical

e.g. You think you're going to win the lottery? **Get real**!

Get something off one's chest: confess; tell something that has been bothering one

e.g. You'd feel better when you **get it off your chest** and tell your family what you did.

Get stars in one's eyes: be fascinated with show business

e.g. She **gets stars in her eyes** and wants to go to Hollywood.

Get the ball rolling: start something happening

e.g. I hope this will **get the ball rolling**, and it will bring in some business.

Get the drop on someone: gain an advantage over

someone

e.g. The FBI uses undercover agents to **get the drop on** terrorists.

Get the nod: receive approval

e.g. We **got the nod** from the Mayor to start a casino here.

Get the runaround: get only excuses and delays

e.g. The reporters were **getting only the runaround** from the Mayor's office, and not the truth of the scandal.

Get the short end of the stick: get less than expected

e.g. It was unfair that we **got the short end of the stick** in this lawsuit.

Get the word: receive an explanation from the authority

e.g. The public were disappointed that they still had not **got the word** from the Governor about the shooting of the teenager by the policeman.

Get the upper hand: gain advantage over

e.g. In this debate, he **got the upper hand** over all the other candidates.

Get time to catch one's breath: find time to relax

e.g. Let me **get time to catch my breath** before I take on the next project.

Get to the bottom of: find out the real cause

e.g. The reporters want to **get to the bottom** of the scandal.

Get under someone's skin: annoy, irritate

e.g. Every time I see him, he **gets under my skin**; he is so annoying.

Get wind of: hear about

e.g. I **got wind of** his resignation from his co-workers.

Get wise to: be aware of

e.g. You'd better **get wise to** his lies.

Get with it: hurry up

e.g. **Get with it**; there's a lot to do.

Get worked up: become emotionally disturbed, feel distressed

e.g. Why did you **get so worked up** over this minor matter?

Gild the lily: decorate something that is already beautiful

e.g. Your dress is already pretty; you don't need to **gild the lily** with this piece of jewelry.

Give as good as one gets: give as much as one receives; pay someone back in kind

e.g. I can take care of myself in any situation. I **give as good as I get**.

Give credit where credit is due: give credit to someone who deserves it

e.g. I was not the one who initiated the project; it was him. **Give credit where credit is due**.

Give one an inch, and one will take a mile: give one something and one will ask for more

e.g. The public are never satisfied. If you **give them an inch, they will take a mile**.

Give someone a piece of one's mind: tell someone off; bawl someone out

e.g. I've had enough from him. I'm going to **give him a piece of my mind**.

Give someone or something a wide berth: keep someone or something at a distance.

e.g. That dog is very fierce. We'd better **give it a wide berth**.

e.g. Your Mom is in a foul mood; **give her a wide berth**.

Give someone the third degree: give someone a hard time by asking too many questions

e.g. If I'm not home past midnight, my folks will **give me the third degree** about where I've been.

Give someone tit for tat: reciprocate

e.g. He took my money yesterday. Now I'm going to take his money, **giving him tit for tat**.

Give something a lick and a promise: do something poorly

e.g. I told you to do the dishes. The dishes are still greasy. You just **gave them a lick and a promise**!

Give the devil his due: give the enemy credit

e.g. He's usually not a nice person. I must **give the devil his**

due: he went out of his way yesterday to be nice to my mother.

Give up the ghost: die

e.g. With the blessing from the priest, the man finally **gave up the ghost**.

Go against the grain: go against one's nature or principle

e.g. I won't help you cheat your boss; it simply **goes against the grain**.

Go ape with: get too excited over something

e.g. These children **go ape with** candies and chocolates.

Go back on one's word: break a promise

e.g. **Going back on your word** does not make you a trustworthy person.

Go ballistic: fly into a rage; be over enthusiastic

e.g. After she heard the bad news, she **went ballistic** and was uncontrollable.

Go bananas: be mildly crazy over

e.g. I thought you'd **go bananas** over the thought of going on a cruise.

Go Dutch: pay for one's own expenses

e.g. Let's have a celebration and enjoy a good dinner. We'll **go Dutch.**

Go for broke: make great effort; risk everything

e.g. To win his re-election, the Mayor would **go for broke**.

Go into a tailspin: fall apart

e.g. After his wife died, his world fell apart, and he **went into a tailspin**.

Go off the deep end: become deeply involved before one is ready

e.g. I know you want to retire. But don't **go off the deep end** before you're financially ready.

Go on the wagon: no longer drink alcohol

e.g. Alcohol is no good for you; time to **go on the wagon**!

Go overboard: be extravagant; do too much

e.g. I know every item is on sale. But don't **go overboard**!

e.g. He needs your help. But don't **go overboard**; after all, it is his project.

Go postal: lose temper, usually due to workplace stress

e.g. If your boss finds out that you are going online during your work, he will **go postal**.

Go south: break down; disappear

e.g. I could not call you: my cell phone **went south**.

e.g. The passenger plane **had gone south**, and was out of the radar.

Go the distance: do the whole amount or the whole thing

e.g. This is a long distance race; I hope I can **go the**

distance.

e.g. This is a long, complicated project. To succeed, you must **go the distance**.

Go through the roof: become very angry

e.g. When he found out that you took his money, he **went through the roof**.

Go to the dogs: deteriorate, go to ruin

e.g. If you don't take care of your house, it will soon **go to the dogs**.

Go to the wall: be defeated after being pushed to the extreme

e.g. The company **went to the wall**, failing one project after another.

Go west: die; fail

e.g. The last Vietnam veteran **had gone west**.

Gravy: easy profit; extra money

e.g. After the expenses, the rest is pure **gravy**.

Grin and bear it: endure something unpleasant

e.g. Life is not a bed of roses. Sometimes during difficult times you have to **grin and bear it**.

"H"

Had better: ought to; should

e.g. You **had better** finish your homework before going to bed.

Half a mind: a thought about something but without specific details

e.g. I have **half a mind** to close the store since the business has not been good.

Hamburger: a worthless person

e.g. Your so-called "friend" is no more than a **hamburger**.

Hammer out: work with great effort

e.g. We tried to **hammer out** a solution to the problem but without much success.

Hand in glove: in very close relationship

e.g. You are **hand in glove** with these government officials.

Hand over fist: very quickly

e.g. He is bringing in customers **hand over fist** through the Internet.

Hands down: easily

e.g. The Mayor won his re-election **hands down**.

Handsome is as handsome does: the action is more important than just the look

e.g. He's not only good-looking but also sincere and honest—**handsome is as handsome does**.

Handwriting on the wall: a warning sign

e.g. If the Governor had seen the **handwriting on the wall**, he would not have adopted those unpopular proposals.

Hang around: keep company with

e.g. If I were you, I would not **hang around** with those gangsters.

Hang tough on something: stick to one's position or principle

e.g. You must **hang tough on** something you believe in.

Hard on someone's heels: following someone very closely

e.g. My dog is always **hard on my heels**.

Has had its day: no longer popular

e.g. This bulky lawn mower **has had its day**.

Have a big mouth: gossip a lot; talk behind someone's back

e.g. I don't like your neighbor: she **has a big mouth**!

Have a close shave: have a narrow escape

e.g. I **had a close shave** this afternoon: I nearly got hit by a car.

Have a feel for: show a natural ability for

e.g. My daughter **has a feel for** classical music.

Have a good mind to: tend to

e.g. I **have a good mind to** tell you the whole truth and nothing but the truth.

Have a heart: be generous

e.g. If you **have a heart**, give much more than this.

Have a lot going for someone: have many things working to one's advantage or in one's favor

e.g. You're lucky! You **have a lot going for** you right now.

Have a lot on one's plate: have too many things to do

e.g. I can't help you right now: I **have a lot on my plate**.

Have a low boiling point: become angry easily

e.g. You'd better avoid her. She is in a foul mood and **has a low boiling point** right now.

Have an ace up the sleeve: have a hidden resource or advantage that could be used

e.g. Don't worry! I **have an ace up my sleeve**: I personally know the Mayor.

Have an axe to grind: have something to complain about

e.g. He is the kind of person who **has an axe to grind**: he is always complaining this or that.

Have clean hands: be free from guilt

e.g. I have nothing to do with this bribery; I **have clean hands**.

Have egg on one's face: be embarrassed by a stupid mistake

e.g. He made a totally wrong prediction about the election. Now he **has egg on his face**.

Have it coming: deserve what one gets

e.g. Failure was unavoidable. What you did **had it coming**.

Have money to burn: have lots of money

e.g. Now that he won the lottery, he **has money to burn**.

Have one's fingers in the pie: become involved in something

e.g. As long as you **have your fingers in the pie**, things will not run smoothly.

Have one's hand in the till: stealing money

e.g. Cash is always missing. I suspect that clerk **has his hand in the till**.

Have one's hands full: very busy

e.g. I **have my hands full,** taking care of your four puppies..

Have one's heart in one's mouth: feel strongly emotional about someone or something e.g. Whenever I hear the national anthem, **my heart is in my mouth**.

Have other fish to fry: have other things to do

e.g. I can't help you right now: I **have other fish to fry**.

Have something hanging over one's head: have something worrying one

e.g. Now that I am approaching 65, I **have my retirement hanging over my head**.

Have something to spare: have something extra or more than enough to give away

e.g. Do you **have money to spare**? I need some for my trip.

Have too many irons in the fire: be doing too many things at the same time

e.g. Because he **had too many irons in the fire**, he did a mediocre job.

Heavy going: very difficult

e.g. Many students find algebra **heavy going**.

Heavy into someone or something: obsessed or preoccupied with

e.g. He was **heavy into** gambling and horse racing.

Hell-bent on: determined

e.g. She is **hell-bent on** buying that dress; you won't be able to change her mind.

Hit a snag: run into a problem

e.g. Our project had to be suspended because it had **hit a snag**.

Hit like a ton of bricks: surprise or shock completely

e.g. The sudden resignation of the President **hit the nation like a ton of bricks**.

Hit the books: study hard

e.g. If you wish to ace your test, you must **hit the books**.

Hit the nail on the head: do or say exactly the right thing

e.g. Your remark **hit the nail on the head**; that was precisely the solution to the problem.

Hit the panic button: become very stressed

e.g. Don't **hit the panic button** every time your daughter's boyfriend shows up.

Hit the spot: be refreshing; be exactly right

e.g. In a sultry afternoon like this, a cold beer really **hits the spot**.

Hold one's end up: do one's part; be reliable

e.g. I know I can count on you; you always **hold your end up**.

Hope against hope: have hope in a hopeless situation

e.g. Many people **hoped against hope** that the war would soon end.

Horse of another color: altogether a different matter

e.g. Putting money in home improvement is different from investing in your retirement funds; it is **a horse of a different color**.

Hotfoot it: run

e.g. I'll have to **hotfoot it** to the shop before it closes.

"I"

If the shoe fits, wear it: if it applies, then pay attention to it

e.g. This scenario may not apply to everyone. But **if the shoe fits, wear it**.

If wishes were horses: if wishes were realities

e.g. She wants a five-karat diamond for her engagement—well, **if wishes were horses**!

I'll say: absolutely; I agree with you completely

e.g. "She's beautiful, isn't she?" "**I'll say**!"

In a big way: obviously, in a great extent

e.g. I can go for a beer **in a big way**.

In a dead heat: finish a race at exactly the same time

e.g. I think these two horses may be **in a dead heat** tomorrow.

In a fix: in a difficult situation

e.g. I found myself **in a financial fix** when I lost my job.

In a flash: instantly

e.g. I'll be back **in a flash**.

In a tight spot: in a difficult situation

e.g. I'm **in a tight spot**: I've no money .

In a vicious circle: in a situation in which the solution will only cause more problems

e.g. Printing more money does not solve the financial crisis; it only puts the economy **in a vicious circle**.

In a world of one's own: distant, detached, self-centered

e.g. It's not easy to approach him; he's always **in a world of his own**.

In bad or poor taste: rude

e.g. Your jokes are always **in bad taste**.

Inasmuch as: because of, since

e.g. **Inasmuch as** they are friends, we can put them in the same room.

In bad faith: without sincerity or good intention

e.g. One should not help others **in bad faith**; it only shows one's hypocrisy and insincerity.

In bad sorts: in a bad humor or mood

e.g. What's the matter with you? You seem to be **in bad sorts**. Is it the weather or something else?

In black and white: official

e.g. I have it **in black and white** that the President will come to this school.

In name only: not actual

e.g. He is the President **in name only**; it's the Vice President who is in control of everything in the company.

In no mood to: not feel like

e.g. I am **in no mood** to talk to you.

Inch along: move very slowly

e.g. Business was **inching along** because of the slow economy.

In concert with: together with

e.g. I can see that your mind is not **in concert with** your body; you look absent-minded and agitated. What's on your mind?

In deep water: in great trouble

e.g. Our company is now **in deep water**; it may even go bankrupt.

In essence: basically

e.g. It was **in essence** a one-man race because the rest of the competitors were not up to standard.

In evidence: obvious, visible

e.g. Your mistakes were much **in evidence**, but you were totally unaware of them.

In fine feather: in good condition; in good health

e.g. With a good night sleep, I am **in fine feather** today.

In full swing: in good progress

e.g. The operation of the company is now **in full swing**, and huge profits are on the way.

In good shape: physically healthy and functioning

e.g. I am **in good shape**; I exercise regularly.

In less than no time: very quickly; instantly

e.g. I'll get back to you **in less than no time**.

In mint condition: in perfect condition

e.g. This is a refurbished computer, but it is **in mint condition**.

In nothing flat: in exactly no time at all

e.g. Don't worry! I'll get you to the airport **in nothing flat**.

In one's birthday suit: naked

e.g. He surprised everyone by coming to the party almost **in his birthday suit**.

In one's book: according to one's opinion

e.g. **In my book**, he is a kind and loving person.

In one's mind eye: in one's mind; from one's perspective

e.g. **In my mind's eye**, you didn't do a good job.

In over one's head: with more problems than one can

handle

e.g. Physics is not an easy subject. I am **in over my head**.

In part: to some degree

e.g. We don't like Cleveland; **in part**, it 's the harsh winter.

In retrospect: look backward

e.g. **In retrospect**, I think you really did a good job when you were with that company.

Ins and outs of something: details to do something right

e.g. Take your time; you need to know **the ins and outs of** this procedure in order to do it right.

In seventh heaven: in a state of great happiness

e.g. He was **in seventh heaven** when he found out he won the lottery.

In the bag: achieved, settled

e.g. Now the whole issue is **in the bag**—as good as done

In the black: not in debt (opposite: **in the red** i.e. in debt)

e.g. "How's you finance?" "Well, I am **in the black**, and not in the hole."

e.g. His accounts are always **in the red** because he does not know how to manage his money.

In the dark: not knowing anything

e.g. The Governor was kept **in the dark** all along until the press uncovered the scandal.

In the doldrums: inactive; in low spirits

e.g. She's having her winter blues, very much **in the doldrums**.

In the flesh: in person; physically present

e.g. The President will be right here **in the flesh** at the community college.

In the gutter: in poverty

e.g. If he doesn't straighten out his life, he will end up **in the gutter**.

In the hole: in debt

e.g. You are **in the hole** because you are a spendthrift.

In / into the know: knowledgeable

e.g. He is a very smart guy. I think he can get **into the know** about the operation of the company before long.

In the limelight: in the center of attention

e.g. The Mayor will do anything to get himself **in the limelight**.

In the making: in the process of developing

e.g. The turn of events was history **in the making**.

In the money: wealthy; in a winning position

e.g. He is **in the money** after his repeated success in the real estate market.

e.g. In the next race, that horse will be **in the money**.

In the nick of time: just in time

e.g. We were held up by the robbers. Fortunately, the police arrived **in the nick of time**.

In the right: morally or legally right regarding an issue

e.g. You were **in the right**, and the judge should not have ruled against you.

In the same boat: in the same bad situation

e.g. You lost your job last year. I was laid off last week. We are now in **the same boat**: looking for employment.

In the wake of: following immediately

e.g. **In the wake of** the election came unrest and social disorder.

In the wind: about to happen

e.g. Everyone was worried because we knew something was **in the wind**.

In the wrong: on the wrong side of an issue

e.g. I got into a car accident yesterday. I was not **in the wrong**: I was hit from behind while stopping at the traffic light.

In there: sincere, likable

e.g. He is a guy **in there**; everybody likes him.

"J"

Jack: money

e.g. I don't have the **jack** ready for you.

Jack around: wasting time and doing nothing constructive

e.g. Don't just **jack around**; do something with your life!

Jamming: excellent

e.g. The performance was **jamming**, and the audience were pleased.

Johnny-come-lately: a newcomer

e.g. She is a **Johnny-come-lately** in our club, and we all like her.

Johnny-on-the-spot: a person who is available when needed

e.g. Here comes **Johnny-on the-spot**! We need you to fix the burst pipe.

Juice up: add life to

e.g. We tried to **juice up** the evening with some alcohol.

Jump at something: take it promptly

e.g. You'd better **jump at** the offer; don't miss the golden opportunity.

Jump out of one's skin: react strongly

e.g. He was so scared that he nearly **jumped out of his skin**.

Jump the gun: act prematurely or too soon; make a false start

e.g. Don't **jump the gun**; get all the facts before you make any decision.

Jump to a conclusion: come to a conclusion too quickly

e.g. It's too early to **jump to a conclusion**; just wait and see how things go.

Just about: almost, nearly

e.g. The job is **just about** to be completed.

Just as well: good that an unexpected problem has come up

e.g. It was **just as well** the customer didn't show up; we didn't have the goods ready for him.

Just one of those things: something that cannot be explained

e.g. I don't know how it happened; it was **just one of those**

things.

Just what the doctor ordered: exactly what is required

e.g. Your financial help was **just what the doctor ordered**.

"K"

Keep a straight face: refrain from laughing

e.g. It's difficult to **keep a straight face** when someone acts so funny.

Keep abreast of: keep up with; keep updated

e.g. As a politician, you must **keep abreast of** what is happening around the world.

Keep a level head: keep calm and sensible

e.g. My mother used to tell me to **keep a level head** under any circumstance.

Keep a low profile: stay out of public notice

e.g. After the scandal, the politician has **kept a low profile**.

Keep a stiff upper lip: remain calm and unmoved by unsettling events

e.g. Despite the tragic events, he **kept a stiff upper lip** and looked emotionally calm.

Keep a straight face: not showing any emotion

e.g. After he heard the news, he **kept a straight face**; nobody knew what was on his mind.

Keep body and soul together: stay alive

e.g. In this country, there are many homeless people who hardly **keep body and soul together**.

Keep late hours: stay up late

e.g. You are tired because you always **keep late hours** and don't go to bed until well past midnight.

Keep one's shirt on: be calm and patient

e.g. Don't get too excited; **keep your shirt on**!

Keep one's weather eye open: be alert and watchful

e.g. Some trouble is coming; you had better **keep your weather eye open**.

Keep one's word: keep a promise

e.g. If you say you're going to pick me up later, I expect you to **keep your word**.

Keep someone posted: keep in touch; keep someone up to date

e.g. When you go to college, I expect you to **keep us posted** every now and then.

Keep something to oneself: keep it a secret

e.g. The gossip I just told you—please **keep it to yourself**, and don't let the cat out of the bag!

Keep something under one's hat: keep something a secret

e.g. Please **keep this under your hat**; I don't want anyone to know about it.

Keep the ball rolling: keep the conversation going; keep an activity going smoothly

e.g. You have excellent social skills; you sure can **keep the ball rolling** with that senator.

Keep up with the Joneses: maintain the same social status as one's friends or neighbors

e.g. Don't buy a Rolex watch just to **keep up with the Joneses**.

Kettle of fish: a mess, an unpleasant incident

e.g. That was a pretty **kettle of fish**: your in-laws and your parents arguing at the party.

Kick around: treat badly and unfairly

e.g. He was sick and tired of being **kicked around** in the company; he was thinking of resigning.

Kick back: relax and enjoy

e.g. Now you just **kick back** and enjoy the show!

Kick in the pants: a setback or rejection

e.g. To him, it was a **kick in the pants** when he found out that somebody else got the promotion instead of him.

Kick the bucket: die

e.g. My parrot **kicked the bucket** yesterday.

Kill the fatted calf: have a great celebration or banquet

e.g. We're going to **kill the fatted calf** to welcome you back.

Kill the goose that lays the golden eggs: destroy something that is a source of fortune

e.g. He is one of our biggest clients; we'd better serve him well, and don't **kill the goose that lays the golden eggs**.

Kill time: waste time

e.g. Stop **killing time**! Get back to work!

Kill two birds with one stone: achieve two goals at the same time

e.g. If we can get the deal done with this client without affecting our relationship with other clients, it is **killing two birds with one stone**.

Kiss and make up: forgive and forget

e.g. Let's bury the hatchet; **kiss and make up**!

Kiss of death: an act that ends someone or something

e.g. The scandal was the **kiss of death** for his career in politics.

Kiss something goodbye: expect or experience loss of something

e.g. You've to **kiss goodbye to** your car: its engine is dead and beyond repair.

Knock around: waste time

e.g. Stop **knocking around** and get to work!

Knock oneself out: exert great effort

e.g. I can see that you have **knocked yourself out** to get this project done. Good job!

Knock someone's socks off: amaze; overwhelm

e.g. Your opening speech **knocked the socks off** the audience.

Know the ropes: know how to do something

e.g. If you don't know how to change your tires, ask him; he **knows the ropes**.

Know the score: know the facts

e.g. You think I'm naïve? I **know the score**.

Know what's what: know what's going on

e.g. I have gone through this before; I **know what's what**.

Know where one is coming from: know someone's intention or motivation

e.g. I **know where you are coming from**; I have been there.

Know which side one's bread is buttered on: know what is best for one

e.g. Your boss told you to do this. If I were you, I would do it. You should **know which side your bread is buttered on**.

"L"

Laid-back: calm and relaxed

e.g. You seem very **laid-back** in spite of what has happened.

Last but not least: last in sequence but not in importance

e.g. Now, **last but not least**, we would like to welcome the new secretary of the company.

Last laugh: succeed in the end despite initial difficulties

e.g. He had the **last laugh** when they found out that he won the competition.

Last word: a conclusive statement; the latest thing

e.g. In matters of foreign policy, the Secretary of State has the **last word**.

e.g. This new phone is the **last word** in electronic devices.

Late in life: in old age

e.g. It was only **late in life** that he became a famous writer.

Late in the day: kind of late

e.g. Don't you think it's **late in the day** to change your tactics?

Laugh up one's sleeve: laugh secretly

e.g. We were all **laughing up our sleeves** when she made a fool of herself in front of the audience.

Law unto oneself: set one's own standards or laws

e.g. The protestors did not follow the rules; they were **laws unto themselves**.

Lay a heavy trip on someone: criticize someone

e.g. Don't **lay a heavy trip on** me; I'm your friend, not your enemy.

Lay an egg: perform poorly

e.g. I hope you won't **lay an egg** when you give your speech this evening.

Lay it on thick: exaggerate blame or praise

e.g. When you said he was the best cook, you were **laying it on thick**.

Lead someone astray: cause someone to do something wrong or illegal

e.g. If you are always in the company of lawbreakers, you may easily be **led astray**.

Lead someone down the garden path: deceive

e.g. Internet scam can easily **lead many people down the**

garden path if they are not careful.

Leap in the dark: action with unforeseeable result

e.g. What you are going to do is too risky—almost like **a leap in the dark**.

Learn something from the bottom up learn something thoroughly

e.g. If you want to understand how the project works, you have to **learn it from the bottom up**.

Leave a bad taste in someone's mouth: leave an unpleasant feeling or a bad memory for someone

e.g. He said something to me at the wedding that **left a bad taste in my mouth**.

Leave no stone unturned: try every possible way

e.g. The police will **leave no stone unturned** to find your stolen car.

Leave someone for dead: abandon

e.g. One of the robbers was shot, and the others **left him for dead** when they saw the police coming.

Leave someone high and dry: leave someone in a helpless situation

e.g. When I was in my financial strait, he didn't lift a finger to help me, **leaving me high and dry**.

Leave someone holding the bag: leave someone to take all the blame

e.g. The manager was responsible for the bankruptcy, but

the assistant manager was **left holding the bag**.

Leave someone in peace: stop bothering someone

e.g. Can you **leave me in peace** and stop bothering me?

Leave someone in the lurch: leave someone waiting for some action

e.g. He cancelled the meeting, but did not inform anyone, and I was **left in the lurch**.

Lend an ear to someone: listen to

e.g. **Lend an ear to** the President and hear what he is going to say.

Lend oneself to something: be adaptable to something

e.g. I can never **lend myself to** public speaking: I am always a nervous wreck when I have to speak.

Let bygones be bygones: forget all past wrongdoings

e.g. After all these years, she will not **let bygones be bygones**: she still holds me responsible for the tragic car accident.

Let grass grow under one's feet: take no action

e.g. You are too lazy, **letting grass grow under your feet**.

Let on: pretend; reveal a secret

e.g. He **let on** that he was hungry, but in fact he was not.

e.g. Don't **let on** that you already heard the gossip.

Let one's hair down: become more frank and honest

e.g. I hope you can **let your hair down**, and tell me everything.

Let sleeping dogs lie: let well enough alone; do not look for trouble

e.g. If I were you, I would forget about it, and **let sleeping dogs lie**.

Let the cat out of the bag: give away a secret

e.g. If you tell him what I told you, you are **letting a cat out of the bag**; he has a big mouth!

Let the chance slip by: miss the opportunity

e.g. I could have married her, but I **let the chance slip by**.

Level with someone: speak honestly with someone

e.g. I'll **level with you**: I think you made a serious mistake.

Lighten up: be less serious or sulky

e.g. **Lighten up**—that's not the end of the world!

Like a bolt out of the blue: suddenly and without warning

e.g. The news came **like a bolt out of the blue**, and everyone was completely taken aback.

Like a fish out of water: awkward; not knowing what to do

e.g. I was **like a fish out of water** when I was suddenly called upon to comment on the Mayor's political scandal.

Like a sitting duck: in an open and vulnerable position

e.g. If you expose yourself, you will be **like a sitting duck** in the enemy's firing range.

Like a three-ring circus: too exciting or chaotic

e.g. The demonstration, like a **three-ring circus**, may turn into a riot.

Like hot cakes: a great commercial success

e.g. We were selling our digital phones **like hot cakes**.

Lie through one's teeth: lie blatantly or unashamedly

e.g. How dare you say I took your money! You're **lying through your teeth**!

Live and let live: do not interfere with others' likes and dislikes

e.g. **Live and let live**, and don't interfere with your children's life choices.

Live beyond one's means: spend more than one can earn

e.g. You are in debt because you are **living beyond your means**.

Live by one's wits: live by being clever rather than just by hard work

e.g. If you want not only to survive but also to do well in this competitive world, you must learn to **live by your wits**.

Live in an ivory tower: live away from reality

e.g. Come on, be realistic, and stop **living in an ivory tower**.

Live out of a suitcase: travel a lot

e.g. I am just tired of **living out of a suitcase** for so many years.

Live within one's means: do not overspend

e.g. You will never get out of debt if you don't **live within your means**.

Living proof: actual evidence or example of

e.g. If you work hard, you will succeed in life. I'm the **living proof**.

Living soul: a person

e.g. I haven't told a **living soul** what you told me yesterday.

Long time no see: not having to see someone for a long time

e.g. **Long time no see**! How are you?

Look as if butter wouldn't melt in one's mouth: pretend to be innocent

e.g. I knew he took the money, but he **looked as if butter wouldn't melt in his mouth**.

Look daggers at someone: give someone an unfriendly look

e.g. She **looked daggers at** me when I mentioned that.

Look the other way: purposely ignore something

e.g. **By looking the other way**, he made the problem worse.

Loom large: is about to happen

e.g. A war in the Middle East is **looming large**.

Lose one's grip: lose control of

e.g. The events happened so fast that the Mayor seemed to have **lost grip of** what was happening in the city.

Lose one's temper: become angry

e.g. Don't **lose your temper** over what your son did; he did it in good faith.

Luck out of something: get out of responsibility by sheer luck

e.g. I wish I would **luck out of** my jury duty.

"M"

Make a bundle: make a lot of money

e.g. She **made a bundle** as a realtor during the real estate boom.

Make a clean breast of: confess everything

e.g. In front of the policeman, the man **made a clean breast of** all the crimes he had committed.

Make a clean sweep of: remove all unwanted persons or things; win many prizes or competitions

e.g. I decided to **make a clean sweep of** my basement for my garage sale.

e.g. This candidate has **made a clean sweep of** all the districts.

Make a go of it: make something work

e.g. The situation is rather bad, but we can still **make a go of it**.

Make a hit: accomplish success

e.g. Her new movie **made a hit** at the box office.

Make a long story short: summarize

e.g. Well, to **make a long story short**, we broke our engagement, and that was it.

Make a mountain out of a molehill: exaggerate the issue

e.g. Stop **making a mountain out of a molehill**; it's not that important after all!

Make a name for oneself: become well known as

e.g. You have **made a name for yourself** as a concert pianist.

Make a nuisance of oneself: be a constant bother

e.g. Don't **make a nuisance of yourself**, and stop complaining!

Make a pitch for: say or do something in support of

e.g. The publisher is going to **make a pitch for** the author's new book.

Make as if: pretend

e.g. You **made as if** you enjoyed the film, but you really didn't.

Make a run for it: run fast to get away

e.g. As soon as the police officer turned his head, the suspect **made a run for it**.

Make a stab at: try to do something

e.g. I knew you would **make a stab at** finishing the project.

Make a stink: complain, criticize

e.g. You don't have to **make a stink** at what I did; I was just trying to help.

Make away with: escape with

e.g. The bank robber **made away with** only $100.

Make believe: pretend to be something or someone that is unreal

e.g. Let's **make believe** that we're loaded with money.

Make cracks about: make jokes about

e.g. It's rude to **make cracks about** her makeup.

Make good money: earn a lot of money

e.g. I hope to **make good money** out of this book.

Make hay while the sun shines: take the opportunity and make the most of it

e.g. Go to school and get a good education while you are still young. **Make hay while the sun still shines**.

Make headway: make progress or advancement

e.g. Despite our effort, we have **made little headway** with our business.

Make light of something: treat something as if it were unimportant e.g. This may become a serious problem further down the road. Please **don't make light of it**.

Make one's day: give one great pleasure

e.g. Your compliment **made my day**.

Make oneself at home: feel comfortable

e.g. Please **make yourself at home**; take off your shoes if you want to.

Make or break: succeed or fail

e.g. This book will **make or break** my career as a writer.

Make someone or something tick: make someone or something function

e.g. My car engine is not working; I don't know **what makes it tick**.

Make someone the scapegoat for something: make someone take the responsibility

e.g. The Mayor would **make his assistants the scapegoat for** his financial failure so that he might still be re-elected.

Make the grade: be satisfactory, meet the accepted standard

e.g. Does this cake I just made **meet the grade**?

Make time with: show romantic interest in

e.g. I can see that he is **making time with** your sister.

Make tracks: move or leave in a hurry

e.g. If you don't want to miss your plane, you'd better **make tracks**.

Make waves: cause unnecessary trouble or problem

e.g. Relax and don't **make waves**! Everything will be okay!

Mean-green: money

e.g. How much of that **mean-green** do you need right now?

Meet someone halfway: compromise

e.g. He settled the agreement with her by **meeting her halfway**.

Melt in one's mouth: taste very good

e.g. This dessert really **melts in my mouth**.

Mend fences: improve poor relations

e.g. I'll try to **mend fences** with my in-laws.

Mend one's ways: improve one's behavior

e.g. You're an adult now; please try to **mend your ways**.

Mess around: fool around; do meaningless things

e.g. Don't **mess around**, wasting your time!

Mind one's p's and q's: pay attention to one's manners

e.g. When you meet the President, you must **mind your p's and q's**.

Mince words: try to avoid giving offense in one's language; speak carefully e.g. Don't **mince words**—say what's on your mind!

Miss by a mile: fail by a lot

e.g. You got an "F" in your test; you **missed by a mile**.

Money is no object: money is not a problem

e.g. Go and plan the wedding; **money is no object**. I'll pay for all the expenses.

Monkey on one's back: drug addiction

e.g. He has had a **monkey on his back** for years, and he should do something about it.

More dead than alive: completely exhausted

e.g. I was **more dead than alive** after fixing the driveway.

More than meets the eye: there is a hidden meaning

e.g. What the Mayor mentioned in his speech has **more than meets the eye**.

Much ado about nothing: a lot of excitement about nothing

e.g. Your plans all turned out to be **much ado about nothing**.

Muddle through: complete something somehow

e.g. She **muddled through** her performance in the piano competition.

"N"

Naked truth: the plain facts

e.g. This is the **naked truth** whether you like or not.

Name of the game: the main goal

e.g. The **name of the game** is winning; we must win this election no matter what.

Near thing: something that almost failed

e.g. The re-election was a **near thing**—I thought we would lose.

Necessary: money

e.g. We can always use more of the **necessary** from our parents.

Neck and neck: exactly even

e.g. They are going to be **neck and neck** in the race tomorrow. It will be hard to decide who will be the winner.

Needless to say: obviously

e.g. **Needless to say**, we were pleased with the outcome of the election.

Neither hide nor hair: no sign of

e.g. The police searched for hours, but found **neither hide nor hair** of the escaped convict.

Never say die: never give up

e.g. The outcome might not be optimistic, but **never say die**.

New lease on life: a new start in living

e.g. After your college graduation, you will have a **new lease on life**.

Nip something in the bud: stop something in its early stage

e.g. The project was **nipped in the bud** due to lack of funding.

No-brainer: something easy to understand or to do

e.g. This math problem is a **no-brainer**.

No can do: impossible

e.g. He asked me for more money. I told him **no can do**.

No end to: no limit to

e.g. Once you have an email address, there is **no end to** the junk emails you will be receiving.

No flies on: very alert, smart

e.g. You cannot trick her; there are **no flies on** her.

No laughing matter: something serious

e.g. Please take it seriously; this is **no laughing matter**.

No strings attached: with no condition or restriction

e.g. I'll give you this smart phone for free—with **no strings attached**.

None the worse for wear: not worse because of use or effort

e.g. I let you use my car. Luckily, when I got it back, it was **none the worse for wear**.

e.g. You worked very hard all day today, but you look **none the worse for wear**.

Not born yesterday: experienced; smart

e.g. Don't take me for a fool! I **wasn't born yesterday**!

Not have a clue: have no idea

e.g. I don't **have a clue** where I lost my car keys.

Not know enough to come in out of the rain: very stupid

e.g. Well, you cannot expect much of him, who **doesn't know enough to come in out of the rain**.

Not know someone from Adam: not to know someone at all

e.g. What does your friend look like? I **don't know him from Adam**.

Not up to scratch: not good enough

e.g. Your work is **not up to scratch**; I'm very disappointed.

Nothing to speak of: nothing worth mentioning

e.g. "Tell us something about your business trip to Europe." "Well, **nothing to speak of**."

"O"

Occur to someone: come to mind

e.g. It never **occurred to me** that I would fail my driving test.

Odd man out: atypical person or thing

e.g. Everybody has a partner here. You're an **odd man out** because you don't have one.

Of all the nerve: how dare

e.g. How dare you talk to me like this. **Of all the nerve**!

Of all things: from all possibilities

e.g. She said she would want to play football, **of all things**, as her career!

Of consequence: important

e.g. Only officials **of consequence** were invited to the seminar.

Off and running: making a good start

e.g. The project is **now off and running**; everything seems to be in order as planned.

Off color: rude, vulgar

e.g. You were not yourself this evening; you were so much **off color** with that indecent joke of yours.

Off duty: not working

e.g. I'm here tonight because I'm **off duty**.

Off one's feed: with no appetite

e.g. I have been **off my feed**; maybe it's the pressure from my new job.

Off the top of one's head: say something quickly without having to think or remember

e.g. I can't tell you the answer **off the top of my head**.

Of the first water: of the best

e.g. The ballet performance was **of the first water**.

On an even keel: balanced, composed, stable

e.g. If you work in the emergency unit, you have to be **on an even keel** all the time.

On board: participating

e.g. We try to get as many people as possible **on board** this important project.

On cloud nine: very happy

e.g. She was **on cloud nine** when she heard that her

daughter had won the piano competition.

On deck: available

e.g. We need many employees **on deck** this Sunday for the festival.

On faith: accepting without proof

e.g. I'll take your word **on faith**.

On high: holding a position of authority

e.g. Whether we're going to get a bonus will be decided by those **on high**.

On one's last legs: very tired

e.g. I'm on my **last legs**; I've to sit down.

On one's toes: be alert

e.g. A policeman has to be **on his toes** all the time when he is on duty.

On pins and needles: anxious; in suspense

e.g. He was **on pins and needles** until he heard the outcome of the surgery.

On second thought: after some consideration

e.g. **On second thought**, I think I'll not go with you.

On someone's head: take the blame

e.g. I don't think all the criticism should be **on his head**.

On target: on schedule

e.g. If everything is **on target**, the project will be completed by the end of next year.

On the go: busy

e.g. In this day and age, most people are **on the go** day in and day out.

On the heels of: right after

e.g. We can expect bad weather next week, with one storm **on the heels of** another.

On the horizon: about to happen

e.g. You don't know what's **on the horizon**; so be alert!

On the house: given away free by a merchant

e.g. Drink as much beer as you can; it's **on the house** tonight!

On the level: fair and honest

e.g. How can I be sure that you are **on the level** with me?

On the mend: getting better; healing

e.g. He was very sick last week, but he is now **on the mend**.

On the move: moving or happening

e.g. Things are really **on the move** in the sales department.

On the QT: quietly, secretly

e.g. He was accused of accepting the bribe **on the QT**.

On the spot: at once, immediately

e.g. The man was gunned down **on the spot** as he got out his car.

On the spur of the moment: suddenly without much thinking

e.g. He decided to take a vacation **on the spur of the moment**.

On the tip of one's tongue: about to say

e.g. The word was **on the tip of my tongue**, but I just could not remember it.

On the wagon: not drinking alcohol

e.g. Don't give me that drink; I'm **on the wagon**.

On thin ice: in a risky or dangerous situation

e.g. If you go ahead without any backup, you will find yourself **on thin ice**.

On top of the world: feeling victorious

e.g. After winning the gold medal, he has been **on top of the world**.

Once in a blue moon: rarely, seldom

e.g. His gesture of generosity was only **once in a blue moon**.

One for the road: one last drink

e.g. Let me have **one for the road**.

One good turn deserves another: a good deed should be returned by another good deed e.g. You helped me once, and that's why I am helping you this time. **One good turn deserves another**.

One man's meat is another man's poison: what is liked by one person may be disliked by another

e.g. You like fried food, but I don't. Well, **one man's meat is another man's poison**.

One's bark is worse than one's bite: one may threaten but may not do much harm or damage

e.g. If I were you, I would not worry about his threat. **His bark is worse than his bite**.

One's days are numbered: about to die or to be dismissed

e.g. The manager doesn't like her. I would say her **days are numbered**.

Open a can of worms: create more problems

e.g. Why don't you clean up this mess before you **open another can of worms**.

Open a Pandora's box: uncover a lot of previously unsuspected problems

e.g. If I were you, I would not look into his past; you might be **opening a Pandora's box**.

Out and about: well enough to go out

e.g. He had been sick the whole month; now he is **out and about**.

Out in left field: offbeat; strange; eccentric

e.g. He is a strange fellow—a bit **out in left field**.

Out of gas: very tired

e.g. After the marathon, I was **out of gas** for days.

Out of hand: without delay

e.g. The offer was so good that we accepted it **out of hand**.

Out of harm's way: out of danger

e.g. We put a fence around the yard to keep the kids out of harm's way.

Out of one's element: out of one's comfort zone

e.g. I am **out of my element** when I have to do any math calculation.

Out of one's depth: beyond one's understanding

e.g. This theory is **out of my depth**: I am confounded.

Out of place: inappropriate; unsuitable

e.g. Your remark at the party was totally **out of place**. What was wrong with you?

Out of proportion: lopsided; of an exaggerated proportion

e.g. Let's be realistic. Don't blow this thing **out of proportion**.

Out of sorts: be irritable

e.g. She is **out of sorts** whenever her daughter's boyfriend shows up.

Out of the blue: suddenly, with no apparent reason

e.g. **Out of the blue**, he made a stupid remark about the

President's speech.

Out of the hole: out of debt

e.g. If you are not careful with your money, you will never be **out of the hole**.

Out of the question: impossible

e.g. Asking for more money from my parents is **out of the question**.

Out of the woods: out of danger, difficulty, or the unknown

e.g. We are still not **out of the woods** yet; work harder!

Out of turn: not at the appropriate time; not in the proper order

e.g. Your request was **out of turn**, and that was why it was turned down.

Out on a limb: in a dangerous or risky position

e.g. If you go against my better judgment, you will be **out on a limb**.

Over and above: in addition to

e.g. **Over and above** his pay and benefits, the CEO was given a private jet.

Over the hump: overcome the most difficult part

e.g. We are now **over the hump**; the rest may be easy.

Over the long haul: eventually

e.g. If you work hard, you will succeed **over the long haul**.

"P"

Paddle one's own canoe: do something by oneself

e.g. You are not much of a help; often times, I've been left to **paddle my own canoe**.

Pain in the neck: annoyance

e.g. You are **pain in the neck**, always complaining about this and that.

Paint the town red: have a wild celebration during a night in the town

e.g. Let's go out and **paint the town red**!

Paper over: conceal or hide some flaw

e.g. Don't try to **paper over** the errors you've made.

Part and parcel: part of

e.g. Suffering is **part and parcel** of life.

Pass away: die

e.g. The actor **passed away** this morning after struggling with cancer for years.

Pass muster: meet a required standard

e.g. Your physical test **passed muster**.

Pass the buck: put the blame on someone else who is not responsible for it

e.g. It was all your fault! Don't try to **pass the buck** to me!

Pass the hat: collect money for

e.g. He is always **passing the hat** for something

Pay one's dues: earn one's reward through hard work

e.g. He worked hard to become the director of the company; he **paid his dues** through hard work.

Pay the piper: receive the punishment due

e.g. You just can't keep on spending without **paying the piper**.

Pay through the nose: pay too much

e.g. I **paid through the nose** for this piece of trash!

Pearls of wisdom: words of wisdom

e.g. Before the new recruits, the Senior Officer gave them some **pearls of wisdom**.

Perish the thought: don't even think about it

e.g. **Perish the thought** of getting away with murder!

Pick up the tab: pay the bill

e.g. Who is going to **pick up the tab**? Not me!

Pickled: drunk

e.g. It only takes a few drinks to get me **pickled**.

Pie in the sky: a future reward

e.g. Are you helping me just because of **pie in the sky**, or are you really concerned?

Pitch in: help and get busy

e.g. We need help for this project; would you like to **pitch in**?

Play both ends against the middle: gain an advantage by pitting people on opposite sides of an issue against each other

e.g. In American politics, it is not common for politicians to **play both ends against the middle** to win their elections.

Play down: belittle; make less important

e.g. The Mayor tried to **play down** the huge deficit incurred.

Play it safe: be on the safe side

e.g. It looks like rain; **play it safe**, take your umbrella.

Play second fiddle: assume a less important position

e.g. I hate to **play second fiddle** to you, who get all the credit.

Play the field: date many different people at the same time

e.g. He wanted to **play the field** while he was still young.

Plead / take the Fifth (the Fifth Amendment to the U.S. Constitution): not to incriminate oneself

e.g. After consulting with his lawyer, he decided to **take the Fifth**.

Poke one's nose into something: interfere with

e.g. I don't like the way you **poke your nose into** my affairs.

Poop out: tire out

e.g. The marathon race **pooped me out**; I could hardly walk.

Pop the question: propose to marry

e.g. Now that you've got the ring; when are you going to **pop the question**?

Pork out: eat a lot

e.g. I like to **pork out** on french fries.

Pound the pavement: look for a job

e.g. For months, I have been **pounding the pavement**; I still haven't got a job!

Pour cold water on something: discourage someone from doing something

e.g. For months, I have been trying to set up a business. But all along, she has been **pouring cold water on** that idea.

Pour money down the drain: waste money

e.g. It's better to declare bankruptcy, rather than **pouring money down the drain**; nothing can revive the business.

Prick up one's ears: listen very closely

e.g. At the sound of the doorbell, the dog **pricked up its ears**.

Presence of mind: clarity of thinking

e.g. Without **presence of mind**, it is impossible to handle one crisis after another.

Promise someone the moon: promise anything

e.g. He will **promise you the moon**, but he never lives up to his promises.

Pull no punches: speak plainly and directly

e.g. The doctor **pulled no punches** and told him that he had prostate cancer.

Pull the rug out: make it difficult or ineffective

e.g. Everything was going fine until he **pulled the rug out** from under me.

Pull someone's leg: play a trick

e.g. Are you serious, or are you just **pulling my leg**?

Pull the wool over someone's eyes: deceive

e.g. Don't try to **pull the wool over my eyes**: I wasn't born yesterday.

Push one's luck: expect good fortune to continue forever

e.g. You were just lucky that they didn't catch you. But don't **push your luck**!

Push someone to the wall: force someone into a difficult or defensive position

e.g. Don't **push him to the wall**! He might even kill you!

Put all one's eggs in one basket: risk everything at once

e.g. If you put all your savings into this business, you are **putting all your eggs in one basket**.

Put in a good word for someone: say something in support of

e.g. I hope you will **put in a good word** for me when you see the manager.

Put on airs: be arrogant

e.g. He always **puts on airs**, and that's why nobody likes him.

Put one's best foot forward: act or appear at one's best

e.g. When you see your in-laws tomorrow, remember to **put your best foot forward**.

Put one's cards on the table: reveal everything

e.g. I have **put my cards on the table**: either you give up drinking, or we are going to have a divorce.

Put one's foot in one's mouth: say something stupid

e.g. I **put my foot in my mouth** when I told him that his sister was fat and ugly.

Put one's nose to the grindstone: work very hard

e.g. I had **put my nose to the grindstone**, but the manager was not even appreciative of my hard work.

Put someone's nose out of joint: humiliate or offend

e.g. He **put her nose out of joint** by not inviting her to the ball.

Put the finger on someone: accuse someone of some wrong doing; inform the police

e.g. You think I took your money? Don't try to **put the finger on** me!

e.g. I'm going to the police to **put the finger on** him.

Put the cart before the horse: do something in the wrong order

e.g. You messed up the procedure by **putting the cart before the horse**.

Put words into someone's mouth: speak for someone without permission

e.g. I never said that; don't **put words into my mouth**.

"Q"

Quick fix: temporary solution

e.g. Taking a pill may be a **quick fix** to remove some of the symptoms, but it does nothing to cure the disease.

Quick on the draw: quick to draw a gun

e.g. Policemen are deemed to be **quick on the draw**.

Quick on the uptake: quick to understand; smart

e.g. He is **quick on the uptake**; you don't need to give him unnecessary details.

"R"

Rack and ruin: decay and decline

e.g. With alcohol and drugs, his health quickly went to **rack and ruin**.

Rack out: go to bed

e.g. What time do you **rack out** ?

Rain check: a promise that an unaccepted offer will be made later

e.g. Thanks for inviting me to dinner tonight. I can't go. Can I have a **rain check** instead?

Rains cats and dogs: rain heavily

e.g. It's **raining cats and dogs**; you'd better stay until it's over.

Rain or shine: no matter what

e.g. She will be there for you, **rain or shine**.

Raise one's sights: set higher goals or standards

e.g. You're still young; **raise your sights!**

Raise some eyebrows: shock some people mildly

e.g. What the Mayor just said might **raise some eyebrows** among voters.

Read between the lines: infer from; get the hidden meaning

e.g. After listening to the President's speech about not involving the nation in the Middle East conflict, you have to **read between the lines**.

Reckon with: deal with

e.g. Death is something that everyone has to **reckon with**.

Rest assured: you can be sure

e.g. You can **rest assured** that you will get back your money invested.

Ride roughshod over someone or something: treat with contempt and disrespect

e.g. Who do you think you are to **ride roughshod over** everyone?

Ride the gravy train: live in luxury

e.g. He sure could **ride the gravy train** now that he got the money.

Right off the bat: immediately

e.g. As soon as he took over the company, he fired the manager **right off the bat**.

Rip-off: something over-priced

e.g. That sandwich is a **rip-off**!

Rob the cradle: marry someone who is much younger than you are

e.g. Are you serious you're going to marry her? I say, you're **robbing the cradle**! She's only half your age.

Rule the roost: be the boss or in control

e.g. **Who rules the roost** at your house—you or your wife?

Run a tight (taut) ship: run an organization in a disciplined manner

e.g. The new manager really **runs a tight ship**, and now everyone comes to work on time.

Run in the family: a characteristic in all members of a family

e.g. Longevity **runs in the family**: they all live to a ripe old age.

Run off at the mouth: talk too much

e.g. I wish you would stop **running off at the mouth**.

"S"

Sadder and wiser: unhappy but getting wiser from the experience

e.g. **Sadder and wiser**, you will learn never to play with fire.

Saddle someone with: give someone too much work or responsibility

e.g. The new employee was **saddled with** many duties and responsibilities.

Save something for a rainy day: save something for future need

e.g. Don't spend all the money; **save some for a rainy day**.

Save the day: produce a good result instead of an expected bad result

e.g. I thought we would lose, but his final scores **saved the day**.

Say uncle: surrender; ask for mercy

e.g. **Say uncle**! You've lost your re-election!

Scratch: money

e.g. I just don't have the **scratch** to come with you.

Screw up: ruin, damage, make anxious, summon or gather

e.g. I **screwed up** my test today.

e.g. I **screwed up** my knee while walking.

e.g. I was **screwed up** by the stress in my work.

e.g. **Screw up** your courage and face your problems!

Second nature: a habit or natural instinct

e.g. Keep on practicing this until it becomes **second nature** to you.

Sell like hot cakes: sell very quickly; be popular

e.g. His new book **sells like hot cakes**; it's going to be on the bestsellers' list.

See eye to eye: agree

e.g. It is difficult to **see eye to eye** with my parents.

Seen better days: in a state of ruin; not in mint conditions

e.g. If I were you, I wouldn't buy this lawn mower; it certainly had **seen better days**.

See red: become angry

e.g. He **saw red** when he found out that you took his money.

See the light: begin to understand

e.g. I had been trying to explain it to him, hoping that he would finally **see the light**.

Seize on: grab

e.g. This is a golden opportunity; **seize on** it!

Sell someone or something short: underestimate

e.g. He is an accomplished musician; don't **sell him short**.

Serve as a guinea pig: be experimented on

e.g. If I were you, I would not take that drug. Don't **serve as a guinea pig**; that drug has yet to be approved by the FDA.

Serve someone right: deserve the punishment

e.g. It would **serve him right**, if he gets caught.

Set in: begin to happen

e.g. Good fortune began to **set in** as soon as they were married.

Set great store by someone or something: have high hopes for

e.g. His parents **set great store by** his performance; they expected him to win the piano competition.

Set one back on one's heels: shock, surprise

e.g. His sudden resignation **set us all back on our heels**.

Set one's mind at rest: stop worrying

e.g. The doctor said he was on the road to recovery. That had **set her mind at rest**.

Set store by: regard something as valuable

e.g. The people **set great store** by the Mayor's good name.

Settle for: accept as a compromise

e.g. We asked for $500 but **settled for** $400.

Short of: lack; other than

e.g. We are now **short of** cash.

e.g. **Short of** screaming, we had no other way to get his attention.

Shot to hell: tired; ruined

e.g. After the trip, he was **shot to hell**.

e.g. My car was **shot to hell** in the accident.

Show one's true colors: show what one is really like

e.g. It is hard to tell what you are thinking. You never **show your true colors**.

Sink one's teeth into something: take a bite of

e.g. It smells so good; I just can't wait to **sink my teeth** into that roast.

Sink or swim: fail or succeed

e.g. I have done my best. Now is the time to launch the project, **sink or swim**.

Sit on one's hands: refuse to give any help

e.g. When we needed your help; you just **sat on your hands**.

Sit tight: wait patiently

e.g. Just relax and **sit tight**!

Sit up and take notice: be alert and attentive

e.g. You are supposed to watch out for anyone coming near the house. **Sit up and take notice**!

Skeleton in the closet: a hidden and shocking secret

e.g. That he was a gay was **skeleton in the closet**.

Sleep on something: think seriously

e.g. I'll **sleep on** what you just told me. I'll give you an answer tomorrow.

Slip one's mind: forget

e.g. It **slipped my mind** that you would be coming with your wife.

Slip through one's fingers: get away from

e.g. The policemen were looking for the killer, but somehow he **slipped through their fingers**.

Small hours: the hours before daybreak

e.g. I can't sleep through the **small hours**.

Smooth sailing: easy progress

e.g. Ever since the new manager came, business has been **smooth sailing**.

So to speak: in a manner of speaking

e.g. The business has been, **so to speak**, smooth sailing.

Speak of the devil: said when someone, whose name has just been mentioned, shows up

e.g. **Speak of the devil**! Here you are!

Speak volumes: indicate a great deal

e.g. His publications **speak volumes** of his contributions to the technology.

Spill the beans: reveal the truth or the secret

e.g. Who **spilled the beans** about the origin of the gossip?

Square peg in a round hole: a misfit

e.g. You just can't get along with anybody, **like a square peg in a round hole**.

Stab someone in the back: betray

e.g. I trusted you as a friend, but you **stabbed me in the back**!

Stand a chance: have a possibility

e.g. You don't **stand a chance** to succeed.

Stand one's ground: stand up for one's rights

e.g. I'm going to **stand my ground**; I'll fight to the end.

Stand on one's own two feet: be independent

e.g. With a good education, you can **stand on your own two feet**.

Stand over: observe or supervise

e.g. I don't like to paint when someone is **standing over** me.

Stand up and be counted: state one's support for a cause

e.g. If you believe in human rights, then **stand up and be counted**.

Standing joke: something that is always funny

e.g. His fat belly is a **standing joke** among his friends.

Start (off) with a clean slate: start off again from the very beginning

e.g. Let go of the past failures, and **start off with a clean slate**.

Steal the show: give the best performance

e.g. He always **steals the show** when he gives a presentation.

Step on someone's toes: offend

e.g. A politician should avoid **stepping on anyone's toes**.

Stick one's neck out: take a risk

e.g. If I were you, I wouldn't **stick my neck out** for that ungrateful friend of yours

Stink on ice: bad, rotten

e.g. I must say your suggestion **stinks on ice**.

Stir up a hornet's nest: create trouble or difficulties

e.g. You have messed up the project and **stirred up a hornet's nest**.

Straight from the horse's mouth: from a reliable source.

e.g. This is no gossip, coming **straight from the horse's mouth**.

Straight from the shoulder: honest and sincere

e.g. This piece of advice is **straight from the shoulder**.

Strike a happy medium: find a compromise

e.g. After months of debate over the budget, the two parties finally managed to **strike a happy medium**.

Strike someone's fancy: appeal to someone

e.g. If you go to an online dating service, you may find a girlfriend who **strikes your fancy**.

Strike up a friendship / relationship with someone: become friends with

e.g. If you are lonely, go out and **strike up a friendship with** someone who shares your interests.

Stuff and nonsense: total nonsense

e.g. Come on! Don't give me that **stuff and nonsense**!

Stuffed shirt: an overtly formal person

e.g. Nobody would like to invite a **stuffed shirt** like your sister to this casual and informal gathering.

Suit yourself: do as you please

e.g. Well, if you don't want to go, **suit yourself**!

Swim against the current: do just the opposite

e.g. As an innovator, he always **swims against the current**.

"T"

Tail end: the last part

e.g. His speech was long, and only the **tail end** was interesting.

Tail wagging the dog: a situation in which a less important part is in control

e.g. In this coming election, the **tail will be wagging the dog**; that is, the minority will decide the outcome of the election.

Take a backseat to someone: let someone take the control

e.g. I'll **take a backseat** and let you run things.

Take a leaf out of someone's book: act or behave in a way that someone would

e.g. She was successful in her business. If you want to do likewise, **take a leaf out of her book**.

Take a nosedive: take a rapid decline

e.g. Last year the company's profit **took a nosedive**.

Take a spin: go for a ride in a car

e.g. Would you like to **take a spin** in my new car after dinner?

Take after: follow the example of

e.g. He **took after** his father, and began his medical career.

Take forty winks: go to sleep

e.g. I'm very tired. I'll go to bed now and **take forty winks**.

Take heart: be confident

e.g. **Take heart**, you may win the race.

Take it or leave it: accept or forget it

e.g. Here's the deal; **take it or leave it**.

Take one's medicine: accept misfortune or punishment that one deserves

e.g. I messed it up; it was all my fault. I'll **take my medicine**.

Take someone for a ride: cheat or mislead

e.g. Don't **take me for a ride**: I wasn't born yesterday.

Take someone for granted: do not take someone seriously

e.g. His wife complains that he always **takes her for granted**.

Take someone's breath away: overwhelm someone with beauty or grandeur e.g. She was so charming that she **took everyone's breath away**.

e.g. The Grand Canyons really **took my breath away**.

Take someone to task: scold, reprimand

e.g. He was **taken to task** by the manager for not taking care of his customers.

Take someone under one's wings: take over and care for someone

e.g. They **took the children under their wings**, and showed them how to take care of themselves.

Take something in stride: accept something as natural or expected

e.g. It was very rude of him to say it in front of his parents. But knowing what he had gone through, they just **took it in stride**.

Take something on the chin: get a direct blow

e.g. The bad news was a shock to me; I **took it on the chin**.

Take something with a grain of salt: have considerable doubt about

e.g. I must say that I'll have to **take your tall story with a grain of salt**.

Take stock: appraise, consider, estimate

e.g. We have to **take stock** of the situation before we make any decision.

Take the bitter with the sweet: accept both the pleasant and the unpleasant

e.g. In life, one must **take the bitter with the sweet**.

Take the bull by the horns: deal with the challenge directly

e.g. This is a very difficult situation, but we must **take the bull by the horns**.

Take the plunge: attempt something, commit oneself to

e.g. They finally **took the plunge** and got married.

Take the stand: be a witness in court

e.g. The lawyer asked the man to **take the stand**.

Take the words out of someone's mouth: say what someone is about to say

e.g. When you said he was dishonest, you **took the words out of my mouth**.

Take to one's heels: run away

e.g. Before the police could come, the thief **took to his heels**.

Take the cake: win the prize; get the result

e.g. You've been working so hard at the project. Now is the time to **take the cake**.

Take the rap: take the blame or punishment for something one is not responsible for

e.g. I'm not going to **take the rap** for something I have not done!

Talk a blue streak: talk a lot and very rapidly

e.g. I didn't understand what he was saying: he was **talking a blue streak**.

Talk shop: talk about business matters

e.g. In a social occasion, you should not **talk shop**; nobody will be interested in your work.

Talk through the hat: talk nonsense

e.g. During the whole evening, your friend had been **talking through his hat**.

Talk until one is blue in the face: talk a great deal

e.g. I **talked until I was blue in the face**, but she would not change her mind.

Tell tales out of school: gossip

e.g. Don't **tell tales out of school**; people will never confide to you.

That's about the size of it: that's how things are

e.g. You've said it. **That's about the size of it**.

That's a good one: that's funny

e.g. Everybody laughed. **That was a good one**!

That's that: no more to be said or done

e.g. I'm not going to give you any money, and **that's that**!

That's the ticket: what is needed

e.g. **That's the ticket**! If you do as I tell you, you will succeed.

That takes care of that: that is settled

e.g. **That takes care of that**, and we're glad the crisis is finally over

The coast is clear: no more visible danger

e.g. I will not leave this place until **the coast is clear**.

The fat is in the fire: the real problem is out

e.g. The police are investigating the disappearance of the money; I think **the fat is in the fire**.

The pot calling the kettle black: an instance of one with a fault accusing another having the same fault

e.g. You're saying that I am late. How about you? You're **the pot calling the kettle black**.

Then and there: on the spot

e.g. As soon as the candidate finished his speech, he was shot **then and there**.

There's no accounting for taste: no explanation why people prefer certain things

e.g. Why would anybody dress like that? **There's no accounting for taste**.

There will be the devil to pay: there will be lots of trouble

e.g. You messed up the plan, and now **there will be the devil to pay**.

The shoe is on the other foot: experiencing the same

things that one caused another person to experience

e.g. If you were to get drunk like I did, you would then understand what it was like to have **the shoe on the other foot**.

Think on one's feet: think while talking

e.g. If you can't **think on your feet**, write down everything on a piece of paper.

Through thick and thin: through good times as well as bad times

e.g. Don't worry! I'll stick by you **through thick and thin**.

Throw caution to the wind: be reckless

e.g. It's okay to take a little chance now and then; but don't **throw caution to the wind**.

Throw good money after bad: waste more money

e.g. You already lost some fortune on the stock market. Don't **throw good money after bad** by investing on the risky bond market.

Throw in the towel: quit; give up

e.g. After failing to win the race in several attempts, he decided it was time for him to **throw in the towel**.

Tie up: engage or occupy in doing something

e.g. He was **tied up** at the meeting, and could not come to the phone.

Tighten one's belt: spend less money

EVERYDAY AMERICAN IDIOMS FOR ESL LEARNERS

e.g. In this strait economy, many people have to **tighten their belts**.

Time hangs heavy on one's hands: time seems to go slowly

e.g. If you are bored, **time hangs heavy on your hands**.

Tit for tat: repayment in kind; likewise

e.g. If you don't help me today; **tit for tat**, I won't help you tomorrow.

To all intents and purposes: in every practical sense

e.g. **To all intents and purposes**, you are the owner of the restaurant now that your father has retired.

To boot: in addition

e.g. The burglar took the computer, and the printer **to boot**.

Toe the mark / line: do the expected

e.g. If you don't **toe the line**, you'll be fired.

To one's heart content: as much as one desires

e.g. He was basking in the sun, enjoying nature **to his heart content**.

To say the least: not to exaggerate

e.g. When she heard the bad news, her heart was broken, **to say the least**.

Totaled: damaged beyond repair

e.g. My car was **totaled** in the accident, but the insurance company would not pay for it.

To the letter: precisely

e.g. If you follow the instructions **to the letter**, you can set up the system.

To the tune of: to the amount of

e.g. To compensate the damage done, we paid **to the tune of** one million dollars

Touch and go: risky; uncertain

e.g. Her conditions were **touch and go** after the surgery.

True to one's word: keeping one's promise

e.g. He was **true to his word**: he returned the car as promised.

Trump up: make up something untrue

e.g. The witness **trumped up** an excuse why he lied previously.

Try someone's patience: do something annoying on purpose

e.g. He deliberately said nasty things to **try his parents' patience**.

Turkey: a failure

e.g. The performance was a **turkey**, and the audience were disappointed.

Turn a blind eye to: ignore or pretend not to see

e.g. The Mayor **turned a blind eye to** his voters' complaints.

Turn a deaf ear to: refuse to listen

e.g. He **turned a deaf ear** to my advice, and insisted on going his way.

Turn tail: run away

e.g. As soon as he saw the policeman, he **turned tail**.

Turn over a new leaf: begin again; start a new life

e.g. After the divorce, he decided to **turn over a new leaf**.

Turn the tide: reverse the situation

e.g. After years of deficit, the company finally **turned the tide**, and made some profit.

Turn up trumps: end well, succeed

e.g. Their relationship turned up trumps, and they were married.

"U"

Under a cloud: under suspicion

e.g. He has been **under a cloud**; the police has been investigating him for some time.

Under one's own steam: by one's own effort

e.g. He cannot succeed **under his own steam**; he needs the support of his family.

Under the circumstance: given the conditions

e.g. **Under the circumstances**, the policeman could use his gun to protect himself.

Under the table: in secret

e.g. Some sort of deal was made **under the table** without letting the public know.

Under the weather: not feeling well

e.g. I have been **under the weather** since I came back from my trip.

Error

120

Under way: already started

e.g. The project is now **under way**; we'll see how things go.

Up a tree: in a difficult situation

e.g. We were **up a tree**: we had no money.

Up in the air: undecided

e.g. Who will win in the coming election is **up in the air**.

Upset the apple cart: mess up something

e.g. I knew he would **upset the apple cart**, and that's why I didn't want him to come.

Up to par: up to standard

e.g. Your performance last night was not **up to par**, and we were disappointed.

"V"

Verge on: be on the border of

e.g. The company **verges on** bankruptcy.

Vested interest: a personal stake

e.g. He showed a **vested interest** in his uncle's business.

Vicious circle: a series of events that create more problems than solutions

e.g. You take drugs to remove the symptoms, but the drugs also cause symptoms that may require more drugs; you are only creating a **vicious circle**.

"W"

Wait for the other shoe to drop: expect more trouble; wait to find out the complete story

e.g. This is just the beginning of the crisis; **wait for the other shoe to drop**!

Walk all over: treat with disrespect

e.g. You just can't **walk all over** everybody as if they were nobody.

Walks of life: different professions

e.g. In this meeting, we have people from all **walks of life**.

Water down: make something seem less significant

e.g. The Governor tried to **water down** the scandal by focusing on other more important matters.

What-it-takes: the necessary skill

e.g. You've got **what-it-takes** to fix our air-conditioner.

What of it?: it's nothing to you

e.g. Yes, I took it from her without her permission, but **what of it?**

Wing it: improvise; do something without any preparation

e.g. I forgot to bring my script for my speech; I think I'll just have to **wing it.**

Wise up: make someone aware of

e.g. I hope I can **wise you up** to your finance: you spend too much!

Wouldn't dream of: cannot imagine or believe

e.g. I **wouldn't dream of** her doing this behind my back.

"Y, Z"

You bet: yes, of course

e.g. "Are you hungry?" "**You bet!**"

You can say that again / You said it: I totally agree with you.

e.g. "He was lying in his teeth!" "**You can say that again!**"

Zero in on: aim precisely on; focus on

e.g. The public's attention began to **zero in on** the Mayor's scandalous love affair.

ABOUT THE AUTHOR

http://www.stephencmlau.com

http://www.booksbystephenlau.com

http://www.wellness-wisdom-newsletter.com

Made in the USA
Lexington, KY
08 February 2018